Baby Animals
CHICK

Angela Royston

Chrysalis Children's Books

First published in the UK in 2004 by
Chrysalis Children's Books
An imprint of Chrysalis Books Group PLC,
The Chrysalis Building, Bramley Road, London W10 6SP

ISBN 1 84458 087 3

British Library Cataloguing in Publication Data
for this book is available from the British Library.

Editorial Manager: Joyce Bentley
Editor: Clare Lewis

Produced by Bender Richardson White
Project Editor: Lionel Bender
Designer: Ben White
Production: Kim Richardson
Picture Researcher: Cathy Stastny
Cover Make-up: Mike Pilley, Radius

Printed in China

10 9 8 7 6 5 4 3 2 1

Words in **bold** can be found in New words on page 31.

Picture credits
Corbis Images Inc: Robert Pickett 6.
Ecoscene: Sally Morgan 5, 21; Robert Pickett 7, 8; Robin Redfern 16; Angela Hampton 24;
Peter Cairns 28.
Natural History Photo Agency: Henry Ausloos 17.
Oxford Scientific Films: 20, 23, 26.
Rex Features Ltd: Greg Williams 4; Sipa 9; Phanie 19; Organic 22.
RSPCA Photolibrary: E A Janes, cover, 1, 2, 11, 25, 27, 29; Geoff de Feu 10;
Joe B Blossom 12, 13, 15, 18; Angela Hampton 14.

NOTE
In this book, we have used photographs of different types of chicken. Each type has feathers of a certain colour and pattern.

Contents

In the nest

This **hen** has laid an egg in her **nest**. Inside the egg a chick is growing.

The mother hen may lay several eggs. Then she sits on the eggs to keep them warm.

Breaking the shell

The baby chickens are ready to hatch. The chick inside this egg has **pecked** through the shell.

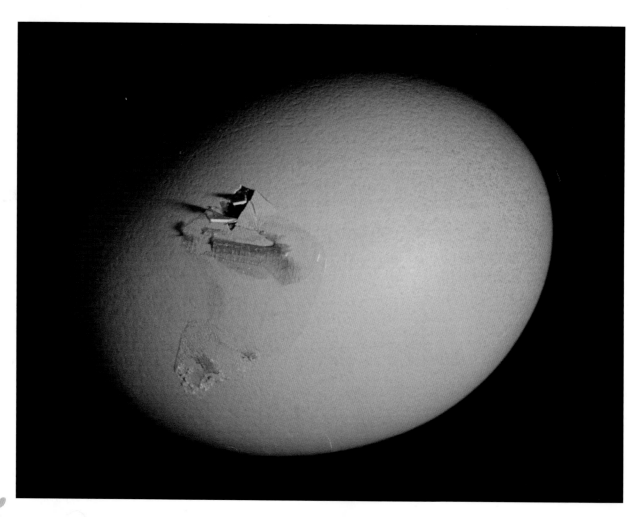

When the hole is big enough, the chick uses its body to push open the shell.

Just hatched

The newly **hatched** chick is wet and very tired. But soon its **feathers** dry.

Not all of the eggs hatch at the same time. This new chick is taking its first look around.

First few hours

Each new chick is covered with soft feathers called **down**. Down keeps the chicks warm.

The mother hen **clucks** softly. The chicks huddle close to her to keep warm and safe.

A few days old

The mother hen pecks for **grain** and other food. The chicks copy their mother.

The chicks soon learn to feed themselves. When they are thirsty, they drink some water.

Sleeping

Each mother hen and her chicks live in a nesting box. The hen comes out first each morning.

At night this hen climbs into her box and the chicks creep under her wings for warmth.

One week old

The chicks follow behind their mother. She watches out for foxes and other dangers.

When she is alarmed, she clucks loudly. The chicks run with her to the nesting box.

Two weeks old

New strong feathers are beginning to grow through the chicks' soft down.

The chicks' **claws** grow strong, too. They use them to scratch the ground for food.

Eight weeks old

The chicks are growing bigger. Now they have long feathers instead of down.

Each chick has a red
comb on its head and a
red **wattle** on its neck.

Ten weeks old

The chicks are old enough to leave their mother and live with the other chickens.

They run around and flap their wings, but they cannot fly more than a few metres.

Perching to sleep

In the evening, the hens and chicks go to the hen house, where they sleep at night.

They **perch** on poles above the ground. They cling to the poles with their claws.

Four months

This young hen is cleaning her feathers. She uses her **beak** like a comb.

The hen needs smooth, clean feathers to keep out the rain.

Five months old

The chicks are now fully grown. This young hen begins to lay her own eggs.

A young male chicken is called a **rooster**. He sometimes calls 'cock-a-doodle-doo!'

Quiz

1 What does a chick use to break through its shell?

2 What do hens and chicks most like to eat?

3 Why do hens need to keep their feathers clean?

4 How far can hens fly?

5 What do we call the brightly coloured flaps of skin a) on a chicken's head b) on a chicken's neck?

6 What sound does a mother hen make as an alarm?

7 How old are chicks when fully grown?

8 What is a young male chicken called?

The answers are all in this book!

New Words

beak hard structure that sticks out from a bird's mouth instead of lips; also called a bill.

claws curved nails on the toes of birds and some other animals.

cluck sound made by a hen.

comb red flap of skin on top of a chicken's head; a toothed instrument for cleaning and straightening hair.

down soft first feathers that keep a baby bird warm.

feather part of a bird's body that covers its skin. Feathers allow the bird to fly and keep water off its body.

grain small seeds, such as wheat, barley and corn.

hatch when a baby bird breaks out of an egg.

hen a female bird, such as a chicken.

nest home of straw or grass made especially for baby animals.

peck when a bird bites with its beak.

perch rest on a pole, branch of a tree or another similar support.

rooster a young male chicken.

wattle red flap of skin on a bird's neck.

Index